CW00847737

Feng Shui

Every Thing You Need To Know About Feng Shui And Applying In Your Own House

Copyright © 2020

DEDICATION

Contents

What Is Feng Shui?

For other uses, see Feng shui (disambiguation).

Feng shui (Chinese: 風水), also known as **Chinese geomancy**, is a pseudoscientific traditional practice originating from ancient China, which claims to use energy forces to harmonize individuals with their surrounding environment. The term feng shui literally translates as "wind-water" in English. This is a cultural shorthand taken from the passage of the now-lost Book of Burial recorded in Guo Pu's commentary.

Feng shui is one of the Five Arts of Chinese Metaphysics, classified as physiognomy (observation of appearances through formulas and calculations). The feng shui practice discusses architecture in terms of "invisible forces" that bind the universe, earth, and humanity together, known as qi.

Historically, feng shui was widely used to orient buildings—often spiritually significant structures such as tombs, but also dwellings and other structures—in an auspicious manner. Depending on the particular style of feng shui being used, an auspicious site could be determined by reference to local features such as bodies of water, stars, or the compass.

Explaining an ancient art and balancing the chi of your home.

When people talk feng shui and trying to make sure their home has the right balance or chi, do we really know what that means? Feng shui is an ancient art and science that was developed over 3,000 years ago in China. The literal translation of "feng" means wind and "shui" means water. In Chinese culture, wind and water are both associated with good health. Thus, feng shui came to mean good fortune. Based on the Taoist vision and understanding of nature, the idea that land is alive and filled with energy, is called Chi.

Feng shui is essentially the interaction of humans and their environments. It enables you to influence these interacting energies to achieve specific life improvements. This influence is gained by positioning or designing your surroundings in harmony with principles of natural energy flow. Feng shui reveals how to balance the energies of any given space to assure health and good fortune for those inhabiting it. These systems of laws for spatial arrangement and orientation are taken into account when people are designing buildings, placing furniture and possessions and even bodies. It offers a unique way of looking at these elements and provides balance, comfort, and harmony into your environment.

The main tools used in feng sui are the compass and the bagua. The bagua, or the energy map, is an octagonal grid containing the symbols of the I Ching, the ancient oracle on which feng shui is based. The Compass , or Luo-Pan, is used to access the deeper information of a building. It consists of bands of concentric rings arranged around the magnetic needle.

It is important to know that there are several different schools of feng shui. Once you master the basics of feng shui you will start seeing powerful results and understand why feng shui is used in both homes and offices all over the world.

History Of Feng Shui

Feng Shui is a tool to help us restore ourselves to our natural state of spiritual beauty. It teaches us ways to bring peace and harmony into our environment.

According to Feng Shui, the places we habitually visit (home and work) are direct reflections of our internal world. This dynamic works in both directions. The more organized, beautiful, and lovely we make our outer world, the more organized, beautiful, and lovely our inner world becomes. By working with Feng Shui, we benefit ourselves and everyone around us. By creating peace and prosperity in our own lives we contribute to peace and prosperity in the world.

Feng Shui and its History

Feng Shui originated 3000 years ago in China. It is the ancient art of placement in our living spaces (homes, gardens and offices). Feng Shui Masters spent their lives learning about aspects of life and how environments enriched or depleted people's Chi' (energy). They studied how to arrange environments to enhance people's lives. Feng Shui is a combination of art and science. From a Feng Shui perspective, not only are we alive in the world we occupy, but all the things around us are also alive with Chi' (energy). The buildings we live in, the land around us, and the furnishings we choose are connected in a dynamic relationship that shapes the quality of our life.

The school of Feng Shui that I choose to practice is called 'Essential Feng Shui'. This school honors the essence of Feng Shui's eastern heritage, while seeking to adapt it to the needs of western culture. This practical approach makes Essential Feng Shui unique. Feng Shui is one of the most beautiful, simple and affordable techniques you can use to enrich your life and living environment.

Chi'

What is Chi'? Chi' is a Chinese word that translates to 'energy.' Chi' is in all things. When our Chi' is depleted (or blocked), our physical body is compromised. The same applies to our outer environments (living spaces). Chi' that moves too fast, or Chi' that is blocked in a living space, will cause challenges and feel uncomfortable for the people who live in the home.

The Bagua

The Bagua is an ancient map of the eight treasures of our lives. It retains the same power and wisdom today that it did 3,000 years ago. Using the Bagua is a great privilege. It provides us with a simple checklist for creating our best intentions in any area of our life. There are nine sectors (guas) of the Bagua. The eight surrounding guas represent the outside areas of our life. They are Career, Knowledge and Spirituality, Health and Family, Wealth and Prosperity, Fame and Reputation, Love and Marriage, Children and Creativity, and Helpful People and Travel. The ninth gua is located in the center of the Bagua. This is considered our inner core, or our center. From our center, everything goes outward. From our outer world, everything goes inward.

Yin and Yang

In our living spaces, we are looking at the Chi' that nourishes us, which Feng Shui concentrates on enhancing. We are always looking to have balance between two extremes which are referred to as Yin and Yang. Yin relates to the feminine qualities such as curved, soft, short, round, etc. Yang refers to masculine qualities such as straight, hard, tall, angles, etc. When dramatic architecture or design becomes extreme, it can result in a Feng Shui nightmare. Exaggerated forms may be viewed as incredible artistic features, however they do not make a cozy habitat for humans. Balancing the Yin and Yang qualities in spaces creates a "just right feeling". This creates harmony and a certain human friendly tranquility is born.

The Five Elements

The 5 elements that are considered the building blocks of everything in our world are: Wood, Fire, Earth, Metal and Water. Feng Shui observes that human beings are made up of the 5 elements. We therefore feel most comfortable when there is a balance of the elements represented in our living environments. In Feng Shui, we seek to create this balance.

Example: Visualize an aquarium.

The aquarium is made up of the 5 elements.

1. We have the glass container and the water that represent water.

2. The plants represent the wood element.

3. The pebbles and rock formations represent the metal element.

4. The fish represent fire.

5. Rectangular or square shapes and earth tones represent the earth element. Most of us feel very relaxed and soothed when

sitting in front of an aquarium.

Feng Shui, the intuitive art of balance and harmony, originated thousands of years ago. Like any other form of art, its history & origin also comprises of many interesting facts. During ancient times, the Chinese shamans, diviners and sage-kings proclaimed the Compass, the Pa-k'ua (eight trigrams), and the Theory of change, as the three building blocks of Feng-shui. As per the legend, the compass was initially used for navigation, during the ruling period of Yellow Emperor in China.

Later, this navigational compass was modified and used in Feng Shui. At the outset of Chou dynasty (1122-207 BCE), King Wen originally employed pa-k'ua to illustrate patterns of change in the natural world. By 8th century BC, Chinese started using the pa-k'ua and the theory of change to encourage the flow of positive energy in a city or a palace. Consequently, the kingdom prospered in harmony and wealth. During the period of Han dynasty (206 BCE-219 CE), the art of K'an-yu, the study of energy carried in landforms, was founded.

The study was supported by the Taoists like Huang-shih Kung and Ch'ing Wu, who said that geological bodies, mainly mountains and rivers, are full of essential energy. Dragon veins are known to be the pathways of energy in mountains, while those in waterways are called

Water dragons. In those times, the Chinese followed this theory on land's energy, not only to make the sites for kingdoms, but for the burial sites as well. The T'ang dynasty (618-906 CE) and Sung dynasty (960-1279 CE) were proved to be the golden periods of k'an-yu.

During the times of T'ang, the geomantic compass (Lo-p'an), along with its twenty-four directions and seventeen rings, was integrated into K'an-yu practice. Yang Yun-sun was the chief k'an-yu master of the period. He was the one, who founded the Three Periods (San-yüan), Three Combinations (San-ho) and Feng-Shui schools. He also conceived that one could chart the energy in mountains simply by looking at the features of contiguous valleys. In the Sung period, Hsü Jen-wang prolonged the idea of 'Three Periods School', to incorporate buildings and landforms.

He founded the Hsüan-k'ung (Mysterious Subtleties) school to evaluate buildings by using the Flying Stars System, which mingles information about the facing direction of a building, the year of its construction and the pa-k'ua in order to trace favorable and unfavorable energies within the building. The Hsüan-k'ung School became popular seeing that cities developed outlying from natural landscapes. The last development phase of Feng-Shui was overlapped by the Ch'ing dynasty (1644 -1911) and the Republic China period (1911-1949).

In the beginning of Ch'ing period, Pa-chai (Eight Mansions) school was established by Jo-kuan and Tao-jen. The theory of Pa-chai is exclusively applicable to residences; it also endeavors to go with the occupant's guardian star. Throughout the Republic years, the Hsüan-k'ung school used the principles of Landform Classification, the compass and the Flying Stars system, to assess the Feng-shui of buildings.

In the same period, the San-yüan school extended to take in the study of residential and commercial buildings. The San-ho school in contrast, remained committed to the study of mountains, valleys and waterways. Acknowledged as the Four Schools of traditional Chinese Feng Shui, the schools of San-yüan, San-ho, Hsüan-k'ung and Pa-chai are still practicing the studies. Infact, today, Feng Shui has become one of the most widely used art forms.

The Basic Principles of Feng Shui

The Chinese words "feng" and "shui" translate to mean "wind" and "water," respectively. This concept derived from an ancient poem that talks about human life being connected and flowing with the environment around it.

What Is Feng Shui?

The philosophy of feng shui is a practice of looking at our living spaces and working environment and striking a balance with the natural world.

In Asian culture, this philosophy is called the Tao, which translates to mean "the way." Taoism is the way of nature and all the basic

14

principles of feng shui reflect nature. Take a look at the essential principles of feng shui: the commanding position, the bagua, and the five elements.

The Commanding Position

The commanding position is the spot in a room that is the furthest from the door and not in direct line with it. It puts you diagonal to the door. Ideally, you should have a clear line of sight to the door.

The commanding position is where you want to spend most of your time when you are in that room. Feng shui guidelines suggest you determine this dominant position in the room, then place your bed, your desk, or your stove in diagonal alignment, if you can. These three parts of your house are critical since each represents an essential part of your life. The bed stands for you, the desk is an extension of your career, and the stove represents your wealth and nourishment.

The Feng Shui Bagua Map

A bagua is the feng shui energy map superimposed on the floor plan of your home. The Chinese word "bagua" translates to mean "eight areas." Each of the eight areas relates to a different life circumstance, such as family, wealth, or career. And, each of these areas has corresponding shapes, colors, seasons, number, and earthly elements. At the center of the bagua—a ninth area—is you, representing your overall health and wellness.

There are several feng shui schools of thought. All of them use baguas when analyzing your home; however, some may apply the bagua in different ways. The Western and BTB (Black Sect) schools usually lay the bagua so that the knowledge, career, and helpful people areas align with the front door of the home. The Flying Stars and other classical schools may orient the bagua based on the energy of the year or the compass.

The Bagua Areas

The easiest way to incorporate the bagua in your life is to identify one to three areas that need the most attention. Do not attempt to work on all areas at once. To strengthen your energy or improve flow in those areas, incorporate feng shui suggestions in that particular area. For example, if you want to encourage fertility, you might add a metallic, circular table in the part of your house representing children.

Family (Zhen)

- Representing: Family, new beginnings

- Shape: Columnar, rectangular

- Colors: Green, blues, teal

- Season: Spring

- Number: 4

- Element: Yang wood

Wealth (Xun)

- Representing: Wealth, abundance, prosperity

- Shape: Columnar, rectangular

- Colors: Purple

- Season: Spring

- Number: 5

- Element: Yin wood

Health (Tai Qi)

- Representing: Health, overall wellness, the center

- Shape: Flat, square

- Colors: Brown, orange, yellow

- Season: Transitions between the seasons

- Number: 5

- Element: Earth

Helpful People (Qian)

- Representing: Helpful people, benefactors, travel

- Shape: Circular, spherical

- Colors: Gray, metallics

- Season: Autumn

- Number: 6

- Element: Yang metal

Children (Dui)

- Representing: Children, completion, joy

- Shape: Circular, spherical

- Colors: White, metallics

- Season: Autumn

- Number: 7

- Element: Yin metal

Knowledge (Gen)

- Representing: Knowledge, self-cultivation, skillfulness

- Shape: Flat, square

- Colors: Dark blue

- Season: Transitions between the seasons

- Number: 8

- Element: Yang earth

Fame (Li)

- Representing: Fame, reputation, passion, visibility

- Shape: Triangle, pointy

- Colors: Red

- Season: Summer

- Number: 9

- Element: Fire

Career (Kan)

- Representing: Career, path in life

- Shape: Wavy, curvy

- Colors: Black

- Season: Winter

- Number: 1

- Element: Water

Partnerships (Kun)

- Representing: Partnerships, marriage, self-care

- Shape: Flat, square

- Colors: Pink

- Season: Transitions between the seasons

- Number: 2

- Element: Yin earth

The Five Elements

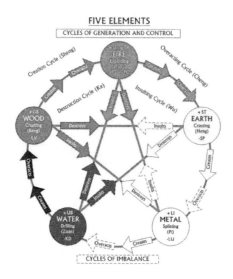

The five elements—earth, metal, water, wood, and fire—come from the Taoist tradition. The elements are five interrelated phases in life that work together to create a complete system. Typically, the practice of feng shui works to balance these five facets in your home and each of your life areas or bagua.

To incorporate the elements in your life and your home, you have to define where you want to focus your energy. Much like the bagua, you choose the one to three areas of your life you want to improve. Then, you strengthen your energy and your home's energy by adding the suggested colors or shapes in that room.

For example, your bagua shows that your bedroom aligns with your health, overall wellness, and the place where you rejuvenate. It ties into the earth element. Consider ways to incorporate earth tones, ceramic or clay pottery, stones, or crystals in that room. After you have made improvements there, focus on a couple of other rooms or areas of your life. Look at the corresponding elements in those rooms and welcome that positive change into your life by adding those elements. The intent is to bring positive energy to those rooms, those areas of your life, and, ultimately, your entire home.

Earth

- Qualities: Grounded, self-care, stable

- Shape: Flat, square

- Colors: Brown, orange, yellow

- Season: Transitions between the seasons

- Areas: Health, knowledge, partnerships

Metal

- Qualities: Efficient, precise, beauty

- Shape: Circular, spherical

- Colors: White, metallics

- Season: Autumn

- Areas: Helpful people, children

Water

- Qualities: Downward, flowing, shifting

- Shape: Wavy, curvy

- Colors: Black

- Season: Winter

- Area: Career

Wood

- Qualities: Expansive, vitality, upward

- Shape: Columnar, rectangular

- Colors: Green, blues

- Season: Spring

- Areas: Family, wealth

Fire

- Qualities: Passion, illuminating, brilliant

- Shape: Triangle, pointy

- Colors: Red

- Season: Summer

- Area: Fame

How to Create Good Feng Shui in Your Home

It can be overwhelming trying to figure out where to start when it comes to cultivating good feng shui in your home. What rooms should you begin with? How do you start fresh or what do you do if a room is already decorated?

5 Easy Ways to Create Good Feng Shui in Your Home

Thankfully, it doesn't need to be challenging. We've compiled a few ideas that will kickstart your journey to a happier and healthier home. So whether you're new to feng shui or an expert, here are nine essential steps to create good feng shui in every room of your home.

1. Brighten Up Your Entry

In feng shui, your entry represents how energy enters your home and your life. We say the front door is the "mouth of qi." Naturally, the entry is first place to start when you want to create good feng shui in your home.

Start with decluttering and removing any debris. A lot of objects tend to accumulate at the front door. I'm not saying it needs to be completely empty, but rather uncluttered. Make it work for you.

Next, sweep and clean up the area. The front entry (interior and exterior) is often overlooked. Wipe down the door and shake out the door mat. Take a good look around.

Then can you make this space more inviting and spacious by removing or adding anything. This creates a place for the energy that enters your home to collect and gather.

Finally, make sure this space is well lit and bright. Add lighting or change the bulbs.

2. Clean Your Windows

Windows symbolize the eyes of the adults in the home. For children, they symbolize their voice. To create good feng shui in your home, clean your windows on a regular basis. Clear, clean windows let in more sunlight.

Sunlight naturally energizes and wakes us up. Sunlight also vibrantly renders all of the colors and objects that we see. Therefore, our homes become more expansive, vibrant, and energetic when we let in more light. Clean windows metaphorically wake us up to see the world around us with the most color, clarity, and precision.

As a bonus, use non-toxic cleaners whenever possible. One of our favorites is a simple solution of white vinegar, water, and a few drops of essential oil.

3. Give Your Doors Some Attention

In feng shui, doors represent your voice and communication. Doors are also portals in which opportunities can come into your life. This is why your doors deserve a bit of your attention.

There are two things to look out for. First, be sure that all your doors can open to at least a full 90 degrees. When there is a bunch of clutter behind a door, it can't open all the way. This means that you're only able to receive a portion of the opportunities life has to offer. There's parts that you're closing yourself off to.

Second, check that all your doors are working properly. Make sure that the hardware functions effortlessly and the hinges are not squeaking. Look to see that the door can close well and with ease. All these details affect how the energy finds its way to you. You want the flow to be as smooth as possible.

4. Commanding Position

One of the most important principles in feng shui is the commanding position. This governs how you can position yourself in life. Be sure to apply this principle to your to the location of your bed, desk, and stove.

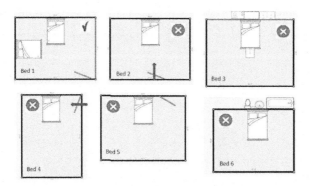

The bed represents you. The desk represents your career. And the stove represents your wealth. When you are in these spaces, be sure that you can see the door without being directly in line with it. For example, when you are lying in bed, sitting at your desk, or cooking at

31

the stove, you want to be able to see the door. Oftentimes this means you end up diagonal or "kitty-corner" from the door.

When you are in a commanding position, you are in command of your life. You are in a position to receive positive energy and the best opportunities.

5. Remove Obstacles in Your Path

Take a good look at your daily path through your home. Yep, we're asking you to literally look at the physical path you walk as you move through your home. From when you wake up and arise from bed, then to the bathroom, and so on as you head out the door. Then from when you get home, make dinner, and end back in bed.

We become desensitized to all the blocks and physical obstacles we have in our daily path. Maybe it's that light fixture that flickers or the door that always sticks and you have to slam closed. It's an obstacle when you have to squeeze through a cluttered hallway. When you hopelessly peer into a closet jammed with clothes that don't fit you anymore—all of this affects you! Like plaque in our arteries, over time these obstacles can accumulate and create problems for us.

The first step is to notice the obstacles, then adjust with kindness. Be gentle. One thing at a time.

6. Be Spacious

Clutter is often in the same sentence as feng shui, but we'd say that feng shui is less about de-cluttering and more about creating space.

How do you make your life more spacious? Start with your home. Find a physical spot: a drawer, room, corner of the refrigerator, desk—the size doesn't matter—and let go of what's no longer necessary. When you let something go, you create open space to invite a new, fresh opportunity.

And don't beat yourself up if the space gets filled up. It's how the universe works. Life is not static or solid, there is impermanence. We can joyfully dance with the waxing and waning of our humanity. Our open spaces get filled up, then emptied, then filled again. Always be open to a fresh start. Find a new (or the same) corner to release and create some space over and over again.

7. Space Clearing

Hand in hand with being spacious is space clearing. Sometimes in feng shui, we call this a space blessing. Along with the physical space is the energetic space and both can be cleared.

There's a few techniques that you can use. My favorites are smudging with palo santo or diffusing sweet orange essential oil. In need of a simple space clearing technique that requires no materials? Visualize bright white sunlight is filling and cleansing your entire home.

When you space clear your home, try to associate it with a positive intention. Hold an intention of what you want to cultivate and create in your life.

8. Plants Bring Life Energy

In feng shui, plants embody life energy. What does that mean? Well, living green house plants connect us to nature and bring vibrancy into our homes. Green plants are like fresh pressed organic green juice for our homes. Think freshness, health, and vitality.

The most important thing to remember is to find plants that you can care for and are appropriate for the space. For example, take your lighting conditions into consideration. If you're new to plants, try some easy ones like the golden pothos.

9. Offer Gratitude

Last, but not least, offer thanks to your home. Feng shui is a shamanic tradition that believes everything is alive, including our spaces! The same life energy (qi) that animates you, also flows through your home.

Your home is your shelter. Your home gives you a place to rest, nourish, celebrate, and so much more. Offering gratitude to your home is simple. Just speak to your home with a humble heart and say thank you.

Feng Shui Tips

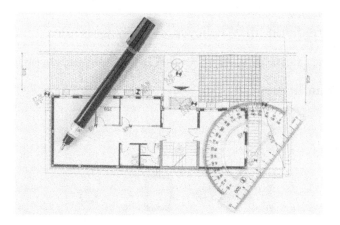

Feng Shui Tips for Bedrooms in All Bagua Areas

In feng shui philosophy, the bedroom is one of the most important rooms in your home. The bedroom represents you! Why? You sleep there, because it's one of the most private rooms in the home, and you spend a great percentage of your life in the bedroom.

When using feng shui to improve your qi (life force energy), it's helpful to overlay the feng shui bagua map over your entire home to determine where the bedrooms are. This can give you insight on the best bedroom location for the members of your household. The bedroom bagua location also offers a perspective on how to decorate your bedroom with consideration to the overall energy of the home.

Follow these step-by-step instructions on how to find where your bedroom falls on the bagua map:

- Orient your floor plan with the front door on the bottom

- Divide the floor plan into a three-by-three grid (like tic-tac-toe)

- Orient the bagua with Gen / Knowledge, Kan / Career, and Qian / Helpful People on the bottom (as shown)

- Overlay each of the nine areas of your floor plan with the corresponding bagua areas

- Determine which bagua area(s) overlap the bedroom(s)

Now what? Once you've figured out where your bedroom falls on the bagua map, read on for tips on how to work with a bedroom in your particular bagua area.

It's also very likely that the bedroom overlaps into more than one area. That's okay! Just like in life, everything doesn't fall into neat little boxes. If possible, work with the bagua area that is covering most of the bedroom. If it's about equal with one or more areas, you have a couple options. You can work with the bagua area where your bed is located (especially for a studio apartment). Or, just check out all the bagua areas and work with the one that applies to you most accurately.

1, Zhen: Family, New Beginnings

This area is connected to family and vitality, so it's a good area for a bedroom, especially for a child or the eldest son.

Ways to enhance a bedroom in Zhen:

- o Accent Colors: Green, blue, teal, navy, black and charcoal

- o Decorate with: Living green plants

2, Xun: Wealth

The Xun area is an ideal bedroom location, especially for the head of the household or an eldest daughter. It's in a strong area of the home because it's in the rear and in a power position.

Ways to enhance a bedroom in Xun:

- Accent Colors: Purple, green, blue, teal, navy, black and charcoal

- Decorate with: Living green plants

3, Tai Qi (Center): Well being

It's pretty uncommon to have a bedroom right smack in the middle of your home, but if this is the case with you, it's not the best feng shui location. It probably doesn't have any windows and might not even be a proper bedroom. The best option is to move to another room. But if you can't do that, try and move your bed over towards another bagua area.

In this case, you would also want to position a mirror on a wall so that it energetically expands your bed and wall into another gua. You do this by placing a mirror on a wall near the rear of the bagua (Xun, Li and Kun). Make sure you can see the reflection of the bed in the mirror.

4, Qian: Helpful People

This is the best location for a guest room, or for someone that's ready to leave the house. A couple examples of this is a temporary guest or a child that's about to move out. It's also a good bedroom if you like to travel and be out of the house a lot. But if it's your bedroom, and you want more stability, it would be helpful to bring in some earth elements to ground your bedroom.

Ways to enhance the stability of a bedroom in Qian:

- o Colors: Earthy and neutral colors

- o Decorate with: Heavy earthy objects like statues, stones or ceramics

5, Dui: Completion, Children

This area is connected to children and joy, so it's a good area for a bedroom, especially for children or the youngest daughter.

Ways to enhance a bedroom in Dui:

- Colors: Earthy and neutral colors, or white and grays.

- Decorate with: Heavy earthy objects like statues, stones or ceramics.

6, Gen: Self-Knowledge

This is the best location for a guest room, or for someone that's ready to leave the house. A couple examples of this is a temporary guest or a child that's about to move out. But if it's your bedroom, it would be helpful to bring in some earth elements to ground you.

Ways to enhance the stability of a bedroom in Gen:

- Colors: Earthy and neutral colors

- Decorate with: Heavy earthy objects like statues, stones or ceramics

7, Li: Fame, Reputation

The Li area is one of the best locations for a bedroom, especially for the head of the household or a middle daughter. It's in a strong area of the home because it's in the rear and in a power position.

Ways to enhance a bedroom in Li:

- o Accent Colors: Green, blue, teal, red and other fiery colors

- o Decorate with: Living green plants, triangles, tall lamps

8, Kan: Career

This is the best location for a guest room, or for someone that's ready to leave the house. A couple examples of this is a temporary guest or a child that's about to move out. But if it's your bedroom, it would be helpful to bring in some earth elements to ground you.

Ways to enhance the stability of a bedroom in Kan:

- Colors: Earthy and neutral colors

- Decorate with: Heavy earthy objects like statues, stones or ceramics

9, Kun : Love, Partnerships

Kun is a good location for a bedroom, especially for the head of the household or a grandmother. It's in a strong area of the home because it's in the rear and in a power position. It's also the area of love and partnerships. If you're single and looking to attract a partnership, use the colors pink or peach.

Ways to enhance a bedroom in Kun:

- o Accent Colors: Pink, earthy tones, neutrals, red and other fiery colors

- o Decorate with: Living green plants, triangles or squares

8 Essential Feng Shui Living Room Tips

Feng shui is more than simply rearranging the furniture in your room.

In fact, feng shui has origins in ancient Chinese principles of balance and environmental harmony. To achieve feng shui in any given room, it's important to create spaces in which you can exist peacefully with your surroundings.

Luckily, maximizing the feng shui of your home doesn't have to be challenging! It's possible to transform your home spaces into areas that can maximize your own well-being - all without breaking the bank or taking too much time out of your day. In this post, we'll address the top feng shui living room tips you can keep in mind as you go about spring cleaning this season!

1. Declutter Your Living Room

The central principle of feng shui lies in spatial harmony. Space is harmonious when everything within it has a purpose and exists comfortably with other objects. Thus, the first step of achieving living room feng shui is to declutter the space itself. Cluttered space can automatically influence your mental health, and not always in positive ways.

It can also disrupt your living room flow. Feng shui is also all about the power of chi, or life force, and its constant motion in and out of the spaces we inhabit. A messy or disorganized living room can automatically inhibit this flow.Begin by removing anything from your living room that is causing clutter. This could mean excess furniture, clothing items, boxes, or even wall decor. Move these items to another room in your home or donate them. Make sure you can move easily in your living room without tripping over things or having to reach for items. This is a good litmus test for achieving a decluttered space.

2. Explore Color Therapy

Color plays a significant role in informing our own psychology. When it comes to feng shui decorating, it's important to work intentional colors into your living room.

Feng shui living room colors may have to do with your room's energy map itself, which we discuss later on in this post. But you can also incorporate colors that automatically invite a sense of balance and flow. Such colors are often on the lighter end of the spectrum. You may begin by painting your living room walls white, for example. Your feng shui decor may include a subtle palette of smooth grays, light blues, pale yellows, and blush. The color green or blue can also signify tranquility and well-being.

Besides painting the walls themselves, you can also use these color suggestions in pillows, furniture, wall art, and rugs.

3. Let There Be Light

Feelings of ease or balance often recall sensations of lightness. Feng shui is all about navigating your environment with respect and grace. As a result, you can achieve living room feng shui by creating a space filled with light. This may mean incorporating large windows-- if you are at the construction phase--or installing gauzy rather than opaque curtains. Pale colored or white walls can also give a living room a sense of lightness, as can lightly-colored hardwood or tiled floors.

You may also want to install a mirror or two along the walls to make your living room feel more expansive. Consider hanging lights, lamps or mirrored furniture, too, for an ethereal lighting solution.

4. Create An Energy Map

To truly target your living room flow, consult a feng shui energy map prior to decorating. This energy map is called a bagua and is designed to help you organize your living spaces with intention.

Using a bagua can be confusing at first. When you consult a bagua, you can identify what elements to incorporate in each of your living spaces, especially your living room. You'll also be more informed about what colors to choose in your living room decor and how to arrange the space to maximize its feng shui.

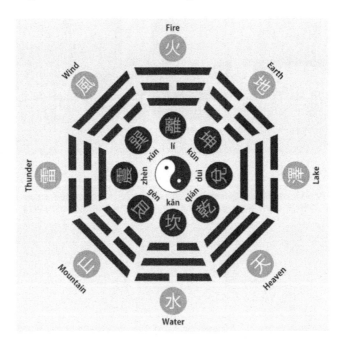

5. Incorporate Functional Furniture

It's difficult to feel harmonious with your surroundings when they don't seem to have a purpose. Because feng shui relies on the power of intention, it's important to be intentional with all items in your living room. This means incorporating functional furniture and getting rid of anything that is superfluous. It's all right to include decorative pieces, but ensure that every item in your living room does have a purpose.

In many cases, this may invite a more minimalist living room design. Minimalist designs often promote greater energy balance because they automatically eliminate clutter. Look for furniture pieces that double in function, such as a bench that is also a storage container. These pieces can make a room feel larger and lighter.

6. Organize Your Living Room

To maintain living room feng shui, keep the room organized and comfortable. Invest in reliable storage solutions that can minimize clutter and free up space. Floating shelves and bookcases are a great way to organize clutter and train the energy of a room to rise upwards. Bookshelves and closet organizers can also help make your living room more comfortable and promote healthy energy flow.

Seeking inspiration? Browse our living room ideas here.

7. Honor the Feng Shui Elements

Whether or not you've consulted a bagua, you can still honor a room's flow by incorporating all of the feng shui elements in the decor itself. These elements include fire, water, earth, metal, and wood.

In general, a balanced home will have an even spread of all of these elements throughout its living spaces. Make sure that your living room honors each element in some way. This may mean simply incorporating the physical elements themselves, such as a metal-backed chair, potted plant, wooden bench, decorative fountain, and candle.

It could also mean acknowledging each element with an image or color.

8. Generate Ease

All in all, your living room's feng shui depends on your own ability to inhabit it with ease and well-being. Feng shui is often a two-way street in this regards.

If your living room currently generates a lot of stress or anxiety, modify the space so that it promotes ease and reflection. This may mean rearranging the furniture, but it may also mean a more drastic change, such as painting the walls or bringing in brand-new decor. Build living room feng shui simply by identifying solutions that will help you move around in a space comfortably and happily.

Feng shui is a powerful principle that can help you live extraordinarily in your own space. Achieve living room feng shui by choosing intentional color schemes, consulting a bagua, and decluttering the room.

Organization and purpose are key factors in a balanced room. Make sure that your decor reflects ease and harmony. Don't forget about the importance of light for your feng shui living room, either.

Feng Shui For Your Target

FENG SHUI TIPS TO IMPROVE CAREER LUCK

In the workplace, some people bear hardships without complaint and struggle for many years but never get a promotion or salary raise; on the contrary, some new to the workplace thrive quickly in the career. Actually, both competence and Feng Shui concern. The Feng Shui of your house and office influences your career. Then, what are the specific Feng Shui elements affecting your career?

Home Feng Shui

Have Backing Inside and Outside the House: it means your house shall have a building or hill behind. For the interior, the headboard shall lean against a wall rather than have nothing behind or face a door or window, and it is same for the study or office chair and sofa in the living room. Without a backing, you cannot get the trust of leadership, and may easily framed up by someone.

Have Protection on Left and Right Side: if the left or right side of your house has no building or is open, you may fail to get support in career. If you are a leader, you might be unable to get the right-hand. If you are an office worker, however, you may have a general relationship with colleagues and customers and cannot communicate smoothly. For the interior of your house, your career will be affected if there is nothing on the left or right side of your office table, sofa and computer chair in your study.

Open and Tidy Front Area: if you want to get the long-term and progressive development in career, the area in front of your house shall be open to get a sound prospect, or you will have no development potential. The walkway outside your front door shall be clean and open for coming in and out freely.

Avoid the Tiny Room: If your room is too small, you will unlikely have a wide field of vision and this kind of layout will oppress you and limit your development in terms of Feng Shui, making it hard for you to get a promotion or development in career.

Avoid a Commanding View of the Interior: for you businessman or politician, you shall avoid a commanding view of the interior after opening the door. It will be harmful if your dining table or bedroom can be seen at the first glance after entering your house, as it means you will be peeped at by someone else and you may suffer financial or political loss, thus cannot enjoy the long-term glory and splendor. You are recommended to set a screen between.

Study Room: elegant and bright light colors shall be used in your study room. The over cold, strong and dark colors will make you feel depressive, which will be unfavorable to your work and study. The small and elegant study room is better than the large but impractical one. If you read or study in a large study room, you will find it hard to concentrate and have your study and career affected greatly. Avoid placing your desk or office table near or opposite the door, or you will face the evil spirit outside directly and suffer from career loss.

Avoid the Beam: if there is a beam above the place you often stay, you will be beset with difficulties in life and have poor physical and mental state, which will affect your career development.

Avoid Making Your Home in Disorder: many people think that the luck for career is only related with the office Feng Shui, so they pay attention to the office Feng Shui but leave their home in a mess. They hardly realize that the home environment is also the key to career achievement. If your home is very messy, the negative energy formed will always follow you and make your luck for career decline constantly, leading to the difficult progress in your career.

Avoid Groundbreaking Right of Your House: if there is a groundbreaking right of the house you are living in, it will lead to the unfavorable conditions and harm your career.

Office Feng Shui

If you pile up sundries on the right side of your office table, your action will be blocked and your vocational vitality will be repressed, leading to disconsideration, salary cut or other problems. To improve your luck for career, you'd better not put anything, especially garbage can, on the right side.

If you sit face to face with your colleague, you will consume the Qi field of each other and it will even cause interpersonal disagreement, and finally affect your luck for success and wealth.

If your office table has something heavy on it, your position and luck for career will be affected.

The position under the beam is extremely suppressed. If you sit in this kind of position and have no choice, you may place Feng Shui mascots like Ding (model of an ancient cooking vessel) or calabash to drive away the evil spirit.

If your table faces a sharp object or corner, you'd better move it because the pattern may lead to fragile body and mind, distraction and no fighting capacity.

Colors

Since East dominates career, you may put some red furniture and decorations in the east to make your family full of vigor and benefit your career;

Yellow is a symbol of wealth and one of the colors dominating the luck for career. Yellow furniture and decorations also can make you get rapid advances in career. Yellow light and tone in living room or bedroom will also work;

Blue is a symbol of pureness, calmness and profoundness which can eliminate the work tension and make you clean-minded.

Improve Luck with East Qi

If you want to get a successful career, or your current career is unsatisfactory, the east Qi can make your career prosperous and positive.

1. Put a bowl in the east of your house or office and fill it with clear

67

Feng Shui

water every morning, to bring you more Qi related to water. Since water and wood in the east generate with each other, it will increase the new Qi in the morning and the effect will be better is the bowl is under the direct sunlight.

2. Put some plants in the east of your office to increase the east Qi because the wood Qi of plants can better import the Qi field.

3. Sit towards east to better inhale the east Qi. Southeast will also be ok if the east is impractical.

Improve Luck with White Crystal

White crystal benefits both health and career. Its energy corresponds to the center of your head, so it can expel the morbid Qi within your body from your sole and make you clear-minded and energetic, thus very helpful to your career and health. For an office table, you may put the larger white crystal column.

FENG SHUI TIPS FOR GOOD HEALTH

68

Health, on the one hand, is subject to your congenital constitution of parental genes; on the other hand, it is affected by the Feng Shui of the acquired living environment. Since the congenital constitution can't be changed, you may learn the Feng Shui of the acquired living environment and adjust it correspondingly to enjoy good health. Then, what are the Feng Shui elements affecting your health?

Light & Humidness

The ill-ventilated houses with poor light, and the dark and damp rooms with basement are not suitable to live in. If you live in the too damp and ill-ventilated house, your immunity will be influenced and you will be prone to depression, cold, chilblain, rheumatism, etc. The over dry air is also adverse to your health and it will make you prone to respiratory diseases and skin inflammation and accelerate the spread of bacteria.

Surrounding Environment

Undoubtedly, the picturesque places are auspicious for you to live from the perspective of surrounding environment. A house with poor surroundings is definitely very bad for your luck and health.

Internal Structure of House

What the front door to the house is the mouth to your body, so the area in front shall be open and well-ventilated. What the living room to the house is the face to your body, so it shall be spacious, bright and unobstructed. Just like your shoulders which symbolize ability and responsibility, the dining room and kitchen shall not be disorderly and unsystematic, or they will increase the pressure of your family. The study and bedroom represent your quality and mood and they shall be solemn. The balcony and sundry room correspond to your arms and legs and the ill-ventilated will make you unable to stretch out.

Room Direction

The directions in your room respectively correspond to the following five elements and body organs: east belongs to Wood and corresponds to liver and gall; west belongs to metal and corresponds to lung; south belongs to Fire and corresponds to heart; north belongs to Water and corresponds to kidney while center belongs to Earth and corresponds to spleen and stomach. When it comes to the corresponding bedroom layout and color, the intergeneration is auspicious. For example, east belongs to Wood and you should not put items in inter-restriction with Wood, such as those items belonging to Earth, Fire or Metal. Instead, you'd better put the lush plants to improve your family's health and longevity or the items belonging to water and landscape paintings, which do also work because Water can cultivate Wood.

Blocked Indoor Piping

In Feng Shui, Water means blood vessel which shall be unobstructed. If there is pipe blockage, leakage or plugged sewer pipe in your house, you may suffer from circulation, respiratory or digestive system diseases.

Bathroom in the House Center

71

In Feng Shui, bathroom is a place of bad luck and other rooms in your house, such as the kitchen, shall stay away from it. A bathroom in the house center is a taboo in Feng Shui because the offensive odors of the bathroom will spread to every corner and have a destructive effect on your family health.

Avoid the High Floor

Do not live too high, or you may absorb less magnetic energy from the earth but more solar energy, which will make you prone to dysphoria, nervous disorder, insomnia, or even depression.

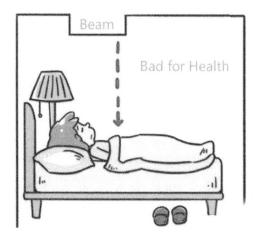

Bed Position

Sleep quality is closely related to health. If you have a beam above the bed, a door opposite the headboard, or a window above the headboard, the direction will be bad for you. Also, if your bed has a bathroom or washing machine upstairs, or your bedroom is at the end of the corridor, your sleep will be affected and you will be prone to cold and headache. Only if you avoid the adverse factors, can you have a sound sleep.

Stacked Stuff under Bed

Some people like to pack up the old things seldom used in daily life and put them under the bed to save space. Since the area cannot be cleaned regularly, the stuff stacked may cause a variety of pests and bacteria. If you sleep above a pile of garbage, you will get the accumulated impact over a long period. In particular, the pregnant woman's bed shall not have stacked stuff under, or the fetus's health will be adversely affected.

Computer at the Bedside

As a matter of convenience, some people like to put the computer at the bedside but the computer will produce radiation and make your head in a radiation environment, which will affect your health seriously and lead to the frequent dizziness and myasthenia of limbs.

Garbage in Front of Door

As the saying goes, disease enters by the mouth. If you put garbage in front of door, you will see it and smell the dirty odor once you open the door, which will affect your health seriously.

Littered Shoes

For the sake of convenience, many families would take off the shoes once entering the front door and put them casually but this is a taboo in Feng Shui. Since you travel around with shoes, there is a variety of bacteria on the shoe soles. If you put them casually, you will take the bacteria into your house and make your family prone to respiratory infection.

Dirty Kitchen

Since food is the first necessity, everyone needs to enjoy abundant meals every day. If the kitchen is dirty and full of dust and lampblack, however, it will have the impact not to be ignored, leading to dyspepsia, or even food poisoning.

FENG SHUI TIPS FOR LOVE AND MARRIAGE

It's not easy for you and your love to get acquainted, fall in love and get married. A harmonious and happy marriage is the dream of every married one. The marriage requires the joint efforts of you and your love to operate and maintain. Besides, Feng Shui also affects your love and marriage and you can change some Feng Shui elements to improve your love and charm, determine or consolidate your marriage and create a good marriage for yourself. Then, how to create a good Feng Shui of happy marriage?

Bed

Bed is crucial to marriage and you should observe carefully to see whether it has the proper position or provokes bad influences. A bed shall be put against the wall rather than face a door, a mirror, and sharp corners or have a beam above.

You'd better put your bed against two walls, at least one wall, rather than make it have nothing to rely on. Putting a bed in the center of the room doesn't conform to the Feng Shui principle.

The mirror in your bedroom shall not face the bed as it may make you haggle over every ounce and sensitive.

The bed shall not face a TV directly, or it may lead it the "dark mirror" effect which will influence your love and marriage. You'd better not put a TV in your bedroom or cover it when you don't watch   it.

The bed shall not be too close to the window, or it may increase the possibility of your lover's illegal love affair.

If the bed is too soft, it will have a bad influence on your health and mentality.

The assembled bed is not suitable for you and your love as it may lead to the emotional estrangement.

Bedroom

The bedroom shall be square, which will make your love more stable and solid and conform to the doctrine of the mean. In this way, you will have an equal and harmonious relationship and a rational thinking on love. Also, it will play a positive role in promoting your love. On the contrary, the long and narrow bedroom in polygon with sharp or oblique corners will make you hot-tempered, impatient or disagree and quarrel with each other.

The bedroom shall be windowed and have soft and elegant lamplight. You can install a master light and spotlights to foil atmosphere in red or purple. If the bedroom has no window to let the sunshine in or the light is too dim, you will have more and more misunderstandings difficult to solve or tend to be unwilling to confide to each other, thus have your love Feng Shui influenced.

The master bedroom shall not have irregular or polygonal items which may lead to disputes, quarrels and conflicts between you and your   love.

Do not put items in disorder; the messy bedroom will lead to discomposure, emotional disorders and unstable love. Also, do not put too many electronic products in your bedroom because the electrical radiation will impair your health and luck in love.

If your bedroom have an en-suite, you should keep the bathroom door closed or put a screen outside the bathroom, or it may lead to the extramarital affair.

If the bedroom is too small, it may lead to narrow mind; on the contrary, it will lead to declined love.

Balance

In home Feng Shui, the left (look out from the door) represents man while the right represents woman and the furniture on both sides shall be in balance. If one side has high furniture while the other is empty or has short furniture, one of you will be mighty and your marriage will be unstable.

Warm Rather Than Coo

When it comes to love and marriage, warm rather than cool items shall be applied. Therefore, you should choose some soft materials for interior furnishing, such as sheer curtain, soft cotton sofa, pink, peach or hyacinthine romantic bed sheet, curtain or quilt which can increase interest and benefit your love and marriage. If you give priority to cool color, it will have adverse impact on your relationship. In addition, the yellow lamplight can create a warm atmosphere.

Avoid Beam

A beam in your bedroom or above the sofa will lead to the unsmooth aura field and unstable emotion, making you often quarrel with each other and have conflicts.

Avoid Sharp Edge

You should avoid sharp edges in your bedroom. Generally, the quarrels between you and your love are caused by the evil spirit in your home. In terms of Feng Shui, you should put away the kitchen knife, scissor or sharp-edged items in time, choose the plants with round leaves, and avoid needle or spiny items which symbolize "the murderous" and will make you restless out of no reason, even quarrel about the meaningless things.

Door

The entry door shall not face the bathroom door directly as it will lead to poor privacy and unfavorable luck with the opposite sex and impose an adverse influence on your love and marriage. The bathroom door facing the bedroom door may also lead to the rough marriage.

Plants and Flowers

Plants in your home not only can purify the indoor air and beautify the environment, but also can avoid evil spirits from the perspective of Feng Shui. After getting married, you can grow some plants symbolizing long love at home, such as lily, orchid and evergreen. Generally, you should put them in the living room, opposite the bed or on the table. However, you should avoid too many flowers, especially dried flowers; too many fresh flowers may lead to the illegal love affair of you or your love while the dried flowers may lead your relationship to decline, thus of great lethality to your relationship. Besides, you should put away the empty vase and the over large or beautiful vase may lead to unfavorable luck with the opposite sex.

Clear Up

Clearing up the items in your home will bring you more space and better Feng Shui. Someone keeps the ex's gifts after getting married but these items bear the marks of previous love and the smell of the ex, leading to the memories of the ex-love. After a long time, these memories will cause the bad moods about the current marriage, even the   unhappy   marriage.

Feng Shui Items

To adjust the Feng Shui of love, you can use the Feng Shui mascots which will improve your relation to a certain degree.

You may have a red or pink fish in a corner of the living room to improve your relationship.

Also, you may put a doll compatible to your zodiac sign at your bedside (left for male and right for female) to benefit your relationship. For example, a Sheep doll for Horse sign and a Pig doll for Tiger sign. (The compatible rule is: Rat and Ox, Tiger and Pig, Rabbit and Dog, Dragon and Rooster, Snake and Moneky, Horse and Sheep)

Rose Quartz and Amethyst have the effect of impove the luck in love relationship. You can wear a rose quartz bracelet or an amethyst bracelet with your zodiac sign to promote love. To place it under your pillow could also help you enjoy better luck in love relationship.

Give Priority to Round

You should give priority to round furniture and furnishing, such as round table, sound and watch. Round can increase your love coagulability and make your love more vibrant.

Items in Pairs

You may put more items in pairs which symbolize mutual love and going with each other all the time. For example, chairs and stools in even numbers, and little ornaments like swans and mandarin ducks in pairs, which will benefit your love. The single items will lead to loneliness in love.

Printed in Great Britain
by Amazon

24175927R00051